D0131334

MVFOL

essential careers

CAREERS IN
AVIATION

SUZANNE WEINICK

ROSEN
PUBLISHING

NEW YORK

Published in 2013 by The Rosen Publishing Group, Inc.
29 East 21st Street, New York, NY 10010

First Edition

Library of Congress Cataloging-in-Publication Data

Weinick, Suzanne.
Careers in aviation/Suzanne Weinick.
    pages cm—(Essential careers)
Includes bibliographical references and index.
ISBN 978-1-4488-8239-7 (library binding)
1. Aeronautics—Vocational guidance. I. Title.
TL561.W44 2013
387.7023—dc23

                                                            2012014433

Manufactured in the United States of America

CPSIA Compliance Information: Batch #W13YA: For further information, contact Rosen Publishing, New York, New York, at 1-800-237-9932.

contents

INTRO

DUCTION

A viation has captivated people's imaginations since the Wright brothers made history with their first successful plane flight in 1903. However, aviation has drastically changed from the early days. Initially, the first pilots entertained people with aerial stunts and gave passengers rides for a fee. As aviation technology improved, airplanes were adapted for military use and then for passenger travel. More instrumentation onboard the aircrafts required more than one pilot in the cockpit. Copilots and flight engineers are needed to operate a modern aircraft.

If the idea of working as a pilot, aircraft mechanic, air traffic controller, or airport management or security officer is interesting to you, then a career in aviation could be your calling. The aerospace industry is in a period of change, and some jobs will be phased out due to new technologies and others will be created.

Modern aircraft cockpits provide the pilot and flight crew with the latest technologies. Round-dial stream gauges have been replaced with digital user-friendly displays that can be tailored to a particular aircraft.

Aviation is an industry that is critical to the country's economy and security. The airline industry has changed drastically over the last forty years. Millions of North Americans fly for business, for pleasure, and to visit family. Commercial airlines are now instrumental in moving products, equipment, and documents around the country and globally on a daily basis. Airlines are more productive and efficient because of new equipment, advanced technology, and a well-trained workforce. However, airlines have a very small margin of profitability. This means that future expansion and improvements to the airline industry will be slow.

Many jobs in aviation require a background in science, mathematics, and engineering. However, there are others that look only for technical training. Cooperative education is a component of many aviation college programs. It provides hands-on opportunities for students to gain practical experience in the aviation industry.

Whether you work on jets, turboprops, propeller planes, or helicopters, all of these aircraft need mechanics to diagnose and fix problems when they arise. Aerospace engineers design, develop, and test new aircraft. In addition, opportunities exist for people interested in making airports and airlines safe. According to the U.S. Department of Homeland Security, 730 million people currently travel on passenger jets each year. That means over seven hundred million bags need to be screened for explosives and other dangerous items. There are high-tech pieces of equipment being developed and implemented at major airports to keep travelers safe and secure.

The aerospace industry, too, has gone through difficult times in recent years because of rising fuel costs, the economic recession, and the downsizing of airlines. However, people will always need to travel for personal reasons, business trips, and relocation. Airlines will need to buy new aircraft and parts, and technologies will need to be added to existing equipment. Careers in the aviation and aerospace industries will bounce back in the future.

This overview of careers in aviation is a guide to a broad range of opportunities from entry-level airport service workers to certified pilots with years of experience. Though there are a variety of careers with different responsibilities within the aviation industry, each requires a similar love for flight. From the ground crew to flight attendants to astronauts, everyone involved in the business has a commitment to aircraft and flight safety. With commitment, passion, and hard work, anyone can soar in the world of aviation.

chapter 1

JOBS IN THE AIR

Aeronautics refers to the aviation systems that operate within Earth's atmosphere. This includes flying the aircraft (planes and helicopters) and the design, manufacturing, and operation of aircraft. Careers in aviation include pilots, aircraft mechanics, and aerospace engineers. When thinking about the aviation industry, there are many jobs that range in educational requirements and earning potential. The following overview of U.S. federal regulation relating to aviation is important to understand because these federal agencies govern the licensing and rules affecting most of the jobs in this field.

The U.S. Constitution gives Congress the power to regulate and control interstate travel by road, rail, and water. In 1926, the secretary of commerce was given the authority to regulate air travel. The U.S. Department of Transportation (DOT) is the federal agency that deals with all transportation issues. The Federal Aviation Administration (FAA) was created in 1958 to create regulations to promote the development and safety of air transportation.

The FAA is the DOT agency that is charged with providing the United States with a safe and effective aerospace system. This includes certifying airlines, airports, pilots, and air traffic controllers in accordance with FAA rules and regulations. The FAA is in charge of setting guidelines for safety relating to aircraft, air carriers and operators, airport regulations, and transforming the nation's airspace system.

The FAA creates regulations as part of the Code of Federal Regulations (CFR) specifically relating to aeronautics and space. The rules pertaining to flight simulation training devices; training of pilots, crewmembers, and ground crew; and air traffic controllers are included in the FAA regulations. More recently, the National Transportation Safety Board (NTSB) was made an independent agency under the Department of Transportation in 1975. The NTSB is responsible for investigating aviation accidents, determining the cause of such accidents, and making recommendations for safety improvements in the aviation field. In an effort to ensure the highest safety standards for the air transportation system, the FAA certifies aircraft from their beginning to their retirement.

Both the FAA and the DOT offer jobs in several areas related to aviation. All jobs with the DOT and FAA require that applicants be U.S. citizens. There are also internships available for college students who are interested in a career in aviation. Specifically, the FAA provides students a chance to develop their professional skills by working for the federal government. The DOT also provides a cooperative education program for high school, college, or graduate students to earn money while exploring careers in aviation or other DOT areas.

Pilots

An aviator is someone who operates an aircraft. To become a pilot, a license and years of training are required. A college degree in aeronautical science can prepare you for a career as an airline, military, or corporate pilot. There are many different types of pilots: commercial pilots that operate passenger planes, freight/cargo pilots, military pilots transporting troops, executive pilots for businesses operating private aircraft, and agricultural pilots flying small turboprop planes to dust crops.

COMMERCIAL PILOTS

An exciting job in the aviation industry is a commercial airline pilot working for a major airline. Commercial pilots who fly for airlines are highly trained professionals. A pilot's office is the cockpit. A pilot needs to learn all the instrumentation, controls, navigation equipment, and electronic communications in the cockpit. Pilots are in charge of flying the plane, but they are also responsible for the safety of the aircraft, all personnel, and passengers, and for the airworthiness of the plane.

More than half of the commercial pilots in the United States received their flight training in the armed services. The other half learned to fly at FAA-certified civilian flight schools. Aeronautical science is the degree offered in some colleges and universities that trains you to be a professional pilot. No matter which route you choose, you must comply with the FAA requirements to become a pilot.

In order to get a commercial pilot's license, you must pass a rigorous physical examination and receive medical

clearance. The FAA requires a minimum of 250 hours of flying time, and the pilot must meet instrument flying and cross-country flying requirements for commercial pilots. Before a pilot can receive an FAA license, he or she must demonstrate

The epaulet stripes on a pilot's shoulder indicate his or her flight experience and level of responsibility. A first officer or copilot wears three stripes and a captain wears four.

flying skill and technical competence. A pilot must pass a check-ride where an FAA examiner requires the pilot to plan a flight and accompanies him or her on that test flight to make sure that the pilot is properly trained and prepared to be a commercial pilot.

FAA licenses carry a rating for the type of plane you can fly, such as single-engine, multiengine, or seaplane. All airline captains have an air transport pilot license. This license requires a minimum of 1,500 hours of flight time.

Commercial pilots employed by the airlines have salaries that range from $45,000 to $110,000, according to the U.S. Department of Labor statistics. Yet, it is a highly stressful job that requires concentration and the ability to work in emergency situations. In addition, the airline industry has been hit hard by the economic downturn over the last several years. Since seniority (number of years at the same job) is how pilots are ranked within an airline, many pilots stay with the same employer to maximize their pay.

SPECIALIZED PILOTS

There are many different types of small airplanes designed to perform special functions. Some of these planes dust crops with chemicals to fight infestation by insects. Bush planes

transport people and supplies to remote regions or isolated wilderness areas. Pilots of these types of planes do not have large salaries or impressive uniforms, but they perform a vital service to those who need them.

Helicopter pilots need many hours of flying experience to land a commercial job. The high-paying helicopter pilot opportunities are generally for sightseeing tour operators, for aerial photography companies, and in medical transportation.

Helicopter pilots are also a unique group of aviators. Since helicopters can hover and land in small spaces, they are used for search and rescue by law enforcement, commuter transport, and traffic reporting. The U.S. Coast Guard uses helicopters to save people stranded at sea or trapped on sinking ships. The military employs helicopters to transport troops and assist in combat missions. One of the most famous helicopters in the world is Marine One, the official helicopter of the president of the United States.

Professional helicopter pilots have special training and must obtain a private or commercial rotorcraft license as required by the FAA. It is costly to take helicopter flying lessons. It could cost between $10,000 and $15,000 to log enough instructional and solo flying time (total of thirty hours) to qualify for a private helicopter license, and it could cost almost $38,000 to $50,000 to secure a professional rotorcraft license. A commercial rotorcraft license requires that a helicopter pilot have a minimum of 150 hours of flying time. According to the Professional Helicopter Pilots Association Web site, to get a job as a professional helicopter pilot, you will need to have over five hundred hours of flying time.

Agricultural pilots, also known as crop dusters, fly over fields to spread crops with pesticides to kill insects. These pilots assist farmers in preventing crop damage. They usually fly small turboprop planes because they can fly slow and low to the ground. Agricultural pilots work for pest control companies or are self-employed. All agricultural pilots must survey the land that they will fly over to check for power lines and other hazards or obstacles that could interfere with their flight path. Agricultural pilots must hold a commercial pilot's license from the FAA, and all states require them to have a license to dispense pesticides certified by the U.S. Department of Agriculture. These types of pilots earn between $30,000 and $80,000 per

JETTING INTO THE FUTURE

A major milestone in aviation came when the jet engine was introduced during World War II. The first commercial jetliner began service in 1952, and the jumbo jet took to the air in 1967. These larger and faster planes gave the airlines the ability to lower the cost of air travel and increase the number of passengers per flight. As the number of flights and aircraft increased, the need to create a system for tracking air traffic became critical. Military jet fighters are the fastest planes ever built, and the pilots that fly them must master the highest skills. The computer systems for these fighter jets cost millions of dollars.

In 1911, Harriet Quimby became the first female aviator in the United States. Amelia Earhart was the first woman to fly across the Atlantic in 1928. Jerrie Mock was the first woman pilot to solo around the world in 1964.

Today, there are over thirty-six thousand female pilots, and more are being added to the ranks through the military. According to Women in Aviation International (WIA), in 2010 there were only a little over 8,200 active female commercial pilots, and only 5,636 of those were certified airline transport pilots able to fly as captain of a jetliner.

year. However, some agricultural pilots are only employed seasonally.

Seaplanes are fixed-wing aircraft that take off and land on water. There are two types of seaplanes: floatboats have pontoons or floats mounted under the fuselage, and flying boats use their fuselage for buoyancy. Rescue organizations, including the U.S. Coast Guard, use seaplanes to help people in remote locations and on lakes. They are also used for sightseeing expeditions in Alaska, Canada, and other wilderness areas. Some seaplane pilots work for charter companies that

Flight instruments in the cockpit provide the flight crew with information about altitude, atmospheric pressure, airspeed, and direction.

provide scheduled service to island resort areas. Some seaplane pilots make around $65,000 per year, but there are very few job openings because there are so few seaplanes in operation.

WHO ELSE IS IN THE COCKPIT?

In a typical large jet aircraft operated by a major airline, there are several airline employees occupying the cockpit. In the left seat facing the nose of the plane is the captain. He or she is the chief pilot who flies the plane, makes all command decisions, and is in charge of the flight's safety. The right seat is occupied by the first officer, who is the copilot. The copilot assists the captain with the preflight duties, including reviewing the flight plan and conducting the preflight check of the aircraft. Some flights have a third person in the cockpit: the flight engineer or second officer. The second officer will monitor the aircraft's systems but will not fly the plane unless there is an emergency. The flight engineer is somewhat of an apprentice on such flights in order to advance his or her flying skills. Newer planes with advanced automated systems make the need for a third person in the cockpit obsolete.

FLIGHT ATTENDANTS

If you like working with people, enjoy traveling, and can handle tight working spaces, you may enjoy being a flight attendant for a major airline. These jobs are in high demand even though

The majority of a flight attendant's duties are related to safety. Flight attendants are required to instruct passengers in the use of emergency equipment and assist them in the event of an emergency.

many flight attendants work long hours (up to fourteen hours per day and longer for international flights). The FAA requires that flight attendants get nine consecutive hours of rest following a duty period. According to the Bureau of Labor Statistics Web site, flight attendants usually fly sixty-five to ninety hours a month, and the average salary is approximately $36,000. Flight attendant salaries are paid based on an hourly rate negotiated by a labor union contract, which is generally based on seniority.

Flight attendants must be certified by the FAA. Attendants must have at least a high school diploma, but many airlines prefer applicants with a college degree. Training to be a flight attendant takes from three to six weeks at a flight training facility. Most major airlines operate their own flight training facilities. Since flight attendants are responsible for the security and safety of the flying public, they learn emergency procedures, including dealing with sick or disruptive passengers and evacuation techniques. Upon completion of the training requirements established by the FAA, a flight attendant will get certified for a specific type of aircraft. In addition, flight attendants must be in good health and be able to reach safety equipment in overhead bins. Individual airlines will conduct background checks on flight attendant candidates and may have additional requirements for employment.

Assignments for flight attendants are based on seniority. This means that newly hired attendants start off placed on reserve status. Reserve attendants must be available on short notice to fill in for another flight attendant who is sick, on vacation, or rerouted. Eventually, they will get regular assignments, but this could take from one to five years (depending on the city of their base airport). Most flight attendants live near major cities where the major airlines have their hubs. If you want to fly internationally, you should learn a second language.

Flight attendants play an important role on commercial aircraft in providing a safe and comfortable flying experience for passengers. Before the plane takes off, flight attendants have preflight duties:

- Direct passengers to their seats and assist with stowing baggage in overhead compartments
- Review safety procedures, point out emergency exits, and explain emergency equipment
- Make sure passengers are buckled in and that all seats are in the upright position
- Prepare for takeoff

During the flight, flight attendants pass out food and beverages to passengers and help with personal comfort needs.

On commercial flights, the FAA requires one flight attendant for every fifty passengers. This provides some job security to friendly individuals who want to see the world but are not interested in being the one flying the plane. A career as a flight attendant may be right for you.

chapter 2

JOBS IN AND AROUND THE AIRPORT

A s aircraft have evolved since the early days of flight, so have the airfields and airports that handle the arrivals and departures. Geza Szurvoy, author of *The American Airport*, points out that airports are an "integral part of our national aviation infrastructure." The U.S. Postal Service began looking toward air transit as a faster way to deliver mail during World War I. Military pilots gained flying experience by carrying mail across the country. However, at that time there were very few airports. The U.S. Postal Service convinced local municipal authorities in strategic locations to build and pay for airports.

Some of the major cities that created airports in the early 1920s were Chicago, Cleveland, and Salt Lake City. The planes could travel only approximately 200 miles (322 kilometers) before they had to land and refuel. Therefore, the transcontinental air routes for the mail connected through communities that crossed the country in the most efficient path available. Boston's Logan International Airport was the first with a hard-surfaced runway that was made in the shape of a "T" so that aircraft could take off in any direction.

In 1936, the Douglas DC-3 was the first commercial airliner that had twenty-one passenger seats and could operate at a profit. This innovative plane transformed air travel into a reliable form of transportation. These higher-performing aircraft required longer runways that would be safe in all seasons. The growing number of passengers flying to their destinations created the need for air terminals that could accommodate them.

The overhaul of the national air transportation system came with the Civil Aviation Act of 1938 and the creation of the Civil Aviation Authority (CAA). The CAA was the independent federal agency dedicated to managing the airway system, aviation safety, and regulating civil aviation in the United States. The Federal Airport Act of 1946 established a program for funding airport construction and upgrading existing ones to meet the needs of an expanding national air transportation system. The responsibilities of the CAA were assumed by the FAA after the Federal Aviation Act of 1958 became law. The FAA was charged with equipping the national transportation system with air traffic control rules and regulations to accommodate the rising number of jet airplanes traveling the U.S. skies.

Fast forward to 1999. The number of airports open to the public in the United States has jumped to 5,314. Regularly scheduled flights arrive and depart from 376 of these airports every day. The FAA classifies thirty-one of these as large-hub, busy commercial service airports.

Cities such as Chicago and Atlanta each have a department of aviation to manage the airports in their jurisdiction. Airports are like any other businesses; they need people to operate the facilities in various capacities. As demand for air travel has increased, airports and airport jobs have grown. Here are some of the positions available in and around American airports.

AIR TRAFFIC CONTROLLERS

Air traffic controllers are responsible for maintaining the safe and orderly flow of aircraft in and around a specific air space. All air traffic controllers are employed by the FAA, and they must first pass the civil service exam and a one-week screening process. The air traffic collegiate training initiative (AT-CTI) program is the educational requirement necessary to become an air traffic controller. The FAA approves AT-CTI programs at many colleges and universities around the country.

Air traffic controllers coordinate the movements of countless aircraft in our skies every day. An air traffic control tower is located at every airport that has regularly scheduled flights.

Air traffic controllers work at airport control towers or one of the twenty-one en route centers (each center monitors a sector of U.S. airspace) around the country. Controllers guide aircraft as they approach or leave airspace surrounding the airport to about 40 miles (64 km) away.

Air traffic controllers advance through different responsibilities in the tower. They monitor aircraft on radar screens. As aircraft fly over radar sites, the data from those radars is communicated digitally via telecommunications lines to controllers hundreds or even thousands of miles away. At the Air Traffic Control System Command Center, controllers plan air traffic for the entire country. The command center controllers communicate with the controllers in the other centers and with the airline dispatchers.

These are some of the different air traffic controller jobs and responsibilities:

- The ground controller notifies the pilot when it is safe to push away from the terminal gate and enter the controlled movement area of the airport (the runways) and instruct the pilot of the aircraft's place in the departure sequence.
- The local controller is responsible for the aircraft until it departs the airport's airspace and it becomes the responsibility of one or more of the twenty-one regional air route traffic control centers.
- The approach controller gets the "handoff" from the en route center and will instruct the pilot on altitude, speed, and flight path adjustments and gives the pilot clearance to land. After landing, the approach controller gives responsibility for the flight to the ground controller.

Air traffic controllers must have knowledge of the instrument flight rules to ensure positive separation between aircraft.

HOW THE 9/11 TRAGEDY CHANGED AIR TRAVEL

Since terrorists hijacked four commercial airplanes on September 11, 2001, air travel has never been the same. During this national crisis, air traffic controllers were given the order to clear the skies over the United States and land all planes. They accomplished that task within 2.5 hours.

In response to the attacks, airport security was tightened and new rules were put in place. Initially, National Guardsmen patrolled the airport terminals. The Transportation Security Administration (TSA) was formed, and a new computer system was designed to prescreen passengers. New technology for scanning people and bags is continually being tested to protect against future threats.

According to Tom D. Crouch, author of *Wings: A History of Aviation from Kites to the Space Age*, the events of 9/11 "sent airlines reeling." By the end of 2001, U.S. and international travel fell approximately 40 percent. Thousands of airline workers lost their jobs, and some airlines went out of business. Aircraft manufacturers felt the effects of the attacks, too, with a decrease in orders for new planes and layoffs of employees.

They communicate with the pilots on weather conditions, speed, altitude, and route. With more than seventy thousand flights a day, air traffic controllers must be alert while performing their duties. It is a stressful job to keep track of numerous aircraft departing, approaching, and passing through a particular air space. Currently, there are over fifteen thousand U.S. air traffic controllers, on duty twenty-four hours a day. There is a mandatory retirement age of fifty-six for air traffic controllers.

The FAA is transitioning air traffic control from a radar-based to a satellite-based system. Satellite technology will allow

Today's pilots enjoy the most advanced technologies, such as the state-of-the-art controls and navigation systems of this Boeing 787 Dreamliner.

controllers to guide aircraft in more direct routes through crowded airspace. Essentially, every controller in the United States will be able to see the exact position of every aircraft flying in an airspace, no matter where they are.

KEEPING THE AIRPORT RUNNING

Airlines tend to hire their own employees, including ticket agents, baggage and cargo handlers, and aircraft maintenance personnel. Airports hire the personnel that coordinate movement at the terminals. Airport service contractors are hired by the airlines or airport to manage and provide certain services to the airline or airport using their own employees. Many of these jobs at the airport require only a high school education. Advancement in these ground service jobs requires hard work and additional training to move up to managerial and supervisory positions. However, each person is instrumental to keeping the airline industry working efficiently.

• Ground service workers are all those airline employees who oversee the loading and unloading of cargo, baggage, and people to and from the aircraft.

- Ramp service workers are the people you see cleaning and maintaining the exterior of the planes at the airports.
- Linepersons and ramp agents meet the arriving aircraft and guide them to the gate. They secure the aircraft, check for leaks, and ready the belt loader (baggage unloader) and other machinery used to unload passengers and baggage from the plane.
- Aircraft fuelers transport aviation fuel to aircraft at the terminals.
- Food service workers are usually employees of a private company that deliver food and beverages for each flight. They also remove any nondisposable dishes and glassware to be cleaned offsite.
- Cabin service workers board the aircraft and prepare it for its next departure once all the passengers leave the aircraft after it has landed and is secured at the arriving gate. With only a small window of time to do their job, these airline employees vacuum, clear trash, clean the bathrooms, and ready the plane for the next passengers.
- Air cargo handlers are responsible for the timely and safe movement of packages and cargo through the airports. Air cargo handlers are the people who use equipment such as forklifts and

conveyors to move air freight and baggage to and from trucks and aircraft. This is a physically strenuous job that requires heavy lifting and working in all types of weather conditions.

- Operations agents are the employees who coordinate all the ground service workers to make sure that each plane that

Ground service workers who guide the aircraft to the proper gate, also called ramp agents, have demanding, yet rewarding, jobs as the ones responsible for the safety of the passengers and crew.

arrives is quickly serviced and prepared for departure. When a plane is delayed in departing, the operations agents must communicate this information to a supervisor so that arriving planes can be informed of new gate assignments and additional information.

It should be noted that many of the jobs described above start out earning minimum wage or slightly higher. There is a high turnover in these occupations particularly because of the low pay and dangerous work environment.

The FAA is also hiring computer specialists to work on upgrading the air traffic control (ATC) automated system that is part of the Next Generation Air Transportation System (NextGen). You need to demonstrate that you have the education and experience working with sophisticated computer systems and that you can handle problem identification, evaluation, and resolution of the ATC computer programs. Salaries for these highly skilled computer specialists start at over $73,000.

EMERGENCY PERSONNEL

Major airports around the United States are operated by states, municipalities, cities, or counties. They employ police, firefighters, paramedics, and security personnel specifically trained for emergency and nonemergency events in and around the airport. Airport firefighters have to have special training to handle hazardous materials associated with aircraft fires. Denver International Airport has the Aircraft Rescue and Firefighting (ARFF) Training Academy where firefighters learn how to handle aircraft fires and aircraft evacuations. Airport emergency personnel must monitor the runways, taxiways, airport terminals, cargo areas, and airport parking facilities. These employees are responsible for the safety of crews, passengers, and airport workers.

AIRPORT CONCESSIONS

The biggest revenue producers for airports are the restaurants, fast-food stands, and stores in the airport concourses. According to Alastair Gordon, author of the *Naked Airport*, "Sales per square foot at airport malls were reported to be three to four times higher than those at normal shopping malls." At Denver International Airport, there are over fifty shops and around forty eating establishments. Airport managers need to coordinate deliveries, manage personnel, and keep the shopping areas clean for the traveling shoppers. These terminal restaurants and stores need employees. Many of these businesses are open long hours (for example, some coffee shops are open from five in the morning to nine at night), so these positions have hours that may meet your schedule.

RESERVATION AND TICKET AGENTS

Whether on the telephone, via computer, or in person, the airline employees who help customers obtain, confirm, and change tickets for air travel are instrumental in making the traveler feel at ease with this stressful process. Commercial airlines hire and train their own reservation and ticket agent employees. Computer skills are a must for these positions, and good communication techniques go a long way toward being successful at this job. The ticket agents who work at airport terminals have additional responsibilities, including determining seating availability, assisting with boarding at the gate, and checking baggage for passengers.

Ticket agents are the face of the airlines as the first professionals that passengers see at the airport. Agents assist with check-in, ticketing, seat assignments, and flight scheduling.

Airlines now offer online scheduling and reservation systems, reducing the need for contacting a ticket agent. However, with airlines consolidating flights, overbooking flights, and rebooking passengers who have missed flights because of delayed connecting flights, the airport ticket counter is still needed to provide customer service. Reservation agents are helpful when planning trips that require multiple flights or frequent-flyer program rewards.

A college education is not a requirement for a reservation or ticket agent, but you should be proficient at using a computer. You may have to lift heavy luggage and you could be required to work nights, weekends, and holidays. You do earn flying benefits as an employee of an airline, and you could advance to a supervisory position. There is a very high turnover rate in this field of work because of the long hours and low pay (starting at $7 to $9 per hour).

CUSTOMS OFFICIALS

Customs officials are federal employees that work for the U.S. Customs and Border Protection (CBP). As of March 1, 2003, this bureau became a branch of the Department of Homeland Security. The CBP officer position consolidates the three positions of customs inspector, immigration officer, and agricultural inspector into one. This means that CBP officers are responsible for enforcing U.S. laws governing imports and exports. But they also report smuggling and revenue fraud and prevent terrorists and weapons from entering the United States.

They determine what goods are admitted into our borders and what, if any, tax or duty needs to be paid upon entry. CBP officers are armed, and they conduct surveillance at all points

Members of the U.S. Customs and Border Protection (CBP), part of the Department of Homeland Security, are responsible for securing the borders and facilitating safe trade and travel to and from the United States.

of entry into the United States. They provide security at airports and make sure that all bags and packages are checked for smuggled contraband or merchandise. They inspect cargo, and they are authorized to board a plane to make sure that the aircraft's manifest matches its cargo. CBP officers must file detailed reports if any customs violations occur.

The CBP has specialized units that perform certain functions. Canine enforcement officers work with trained dogs to search for controlled substances (including illegal drugs). Agricultural specialists inspect fruits, plants, and meats for pests and diseases. Finally, import specialists examine merchandise coming into the country to enforce import quotas and calculate tariffs due.

Customs officers participate in a training program at the U.S. Customs Explorer Academy. CBP officers can be assigned to any of the nine regional territories of the CBP. They work at airports, border stations, seaports, and other points of entry into the United States. The salary for a customs agent is similar to that of a TSA officer. The entry-level employee earns around $25,000 annually.

chapter 3

Aerospace Engineers

Many careers in aviation involve mastering skills in math, computers, and science. Specifically, the design, operation, and repair of aircraft and spacecraft are performed by engineers. Engineering is the branch of science and technology concerned with the design, building, and use of engines, machines, and structures.

In the aviation field, there are two types of engineers: aeronautical engineers who work on aircraft and astronautical engineers who specialize in spacecraft. Aeronautic engineers are then further categorized by their areas of expertise. For example, design aerospace engineers (aerodynamicists) work on the structural construction of aircrafts.

At a minimum, aerospace engineers need to go to college and earn a bachelor's degree in an accredited engineering program. Many aerospace engineers continue their education and get a master's or doctoral degree. In addition, all engineers need to obtain a license after completing their engineering coursework, training as an engineer after graduation, and passing a written exam.

Design engineers transform ideas and concepts into working designs for products that meet a client's specifications for aviation machines. Aircraft electronics and aeronautic design

Aircraft design engineers develop all types of aircraft and their components. These highly skilled professionals use sophisticated software to analyze aerodynamics, aircraft structure, and propulsion systems, among other details.

are concentrations that can lead to a job with an aircraft manufacturing company. Engineers are responsible for the total design of the aircraft, including the shape, performance, propulsion, and operating systems.

Aerodynamicists are engineers that create models of aircraft to see how they perform in a wind tunnel. They also utilize computers to simulate the effect of wind on the aircraft. The information collected will help the team of engineers designing the aircraft determine its speed, fuel efficiency, and aerodynamics.

There are other types of engineers that work in the aviation field. Field service engineers provide maintenance and service information to manufacturers to ensure safe and efficient use of the aircrafts designed. Software engineers create computer software and hardware components to support flight control, display systems, and mechanical and electrical systems in the aircraft. System engineers are responsible for the interface of the complex systems in an aircraft and how they work together during development and maintenance activities. Test engineers perform a complete range of diagnostic tests and analyze the data before the aircraft is set for production. Stress analysts determine how the weight and load of materials used in aircraft behave under extreme conditions of flight.

Aerospace and aeronautic engineers are employed throughout the aviation industry. Many work for government agencies, such as the FAA, DOT, and TSA and for companies that provide parts and services to the airlines and aircraft manufacturers. Other aerospace

Aviation Education

Aviation High School in Des Moines, Washington, is a college preparatory aviation-themed high school. It is the goal of the school to become the premier school of choice for science, technology,

(continued on page 40)

The AIAA is an organization that allows young people to get a sense of the world of aerospace flight and engineering. Its Web site (http://www.aiaa.org) offers comprehensive research on the latest developments, such as new technologies, design contests, and more.

(continued)

engineering, and math in the Pacific Northwest. Aviation High School opened in 2004 and now has a capacity of four hundred students in grades nine through twelve. The mission of the school is to prepare all students for college, careers, and citizenship through a personalized, rigorous, and relevant learning experience that is rooted in aviation and aerospace. The school partners with the aviation and aerospace industries to provide the students with opportunities for careers in these areas.

The American Institute of Aeronautics and Astronautics (AIAA) is a nonprofit membership organization for scientists, engineers, researchers, designers, educators, and aviators. The AIAA has a foundation that sponsors design competitions and student conferences, which provide numerous undergraduate scholarships for students interested in pursuing a career in aviation. Over six thousand students are members of the AIAA and participate in the annual conferences.

Aeronautical technicians perform duties relating to the design, construction, and testing of aircraft, missiles, and spacecraft. There are job opportunities available with federal agencies, such as the CBP, aviation manufacturers, and scientific research and development companies.

engineers work for the U.S. military services or military contractors. The U.S. Department of Defense and the National Aeronautics and Space Administration (NASA) have many opportunities for aerospace engineers. Highly experienced engineers can earn over $80,000 annually for the federal government and even more in the private sector.

Some aerospace engineers work on top-secret military projects. For example, work on unmanned military drones was recently highlighted as an integral part of the U.S. military strategy over the last decade. According to the *Washington Post*, prior to September 11, 2001, the United States "had less than 200 drones, today it has more than 7,000." This industry is in need of engineers that are interested in creating remotely piloted machines for the armed forces.

AERONAUTICAL TECHNICIANS

Aeronautical technicians work along with the engineers and scientists to design, construct, and test aircraft mechanics and equipment. These jobs do not require an engineering degree, but most aeronautical and aerospace technicians have at least a two-year associate's degree or technical institute degree. Entry-level positions are available at aerospace research and manufacturing facilities. Median salaries for aeronautical technicians are around $53,000.

AIRPLANE DISPATCHERS

Once an aircraft leaves the airport, it is the airline's airplane dispatcher who makes sure that the plane is operating safely and efficiently during flight. The pilots confer with the airplane dispatcher by radio transmission to determine the best route to take to the destination. The airplane dispatcher is always checking for changes in the weather and airport congestion. These are the people who decide, along with the pilot, if a particular flight needs to be delayed or cancelled. There are only about 1,500 airplane dispatchers, and they usually have meteorological and radio operator experience. Airplane dispatchers are also licensed by the FAA and complete an FAA-approved airline dispatcher's course.

Entry-level airplane dispatchers earn $20,000 per year, while senior dispatchers can earn around $100,000, according to the Airline Dispatchers Federation. Usually, new dispatchers start out at smaller carriers and hope to move on to a major airline.

chapter 4

AVIATION MAINTENANCE AND SECURITY

F lying airplanes or helicopters is not a career for everyone. However, all aircraft need to be properly maintained and repaired. If you enjoy fixing things and working on complicated equipment, you may be interested in a career in aircraft maintenance. Aviation maintenance technicians (AMTs) learn to repair and maintain aircraft. They need to be trained to diagnose a problem, make adjustments or repairs, and overhaul engines if necessary.

AIRCRAFT MECHANICS

There are over 150,000 aircraft mechanics working for airlines, aircraft manufacturers, independent repair facilities (for repairs on private planes), and in the military. If you are interested in becoming an AMT, you can enroll in an FAA-approved aviation mechanical training program that will provide you with the skills needed to pursue a career in aircraft maintenance. These programs prepare you for the Airframe and Power Plant (A&P) licensing exam that is administered by the FAA. Aircraft mechanics are also required to look for unsafe conditions in an aircraft.

The training program gives the student the knowledge to gain employment as an aviation maintenance technician or aviation maintenance technician engineer. This type of training will also set you up to eventually become an aviation

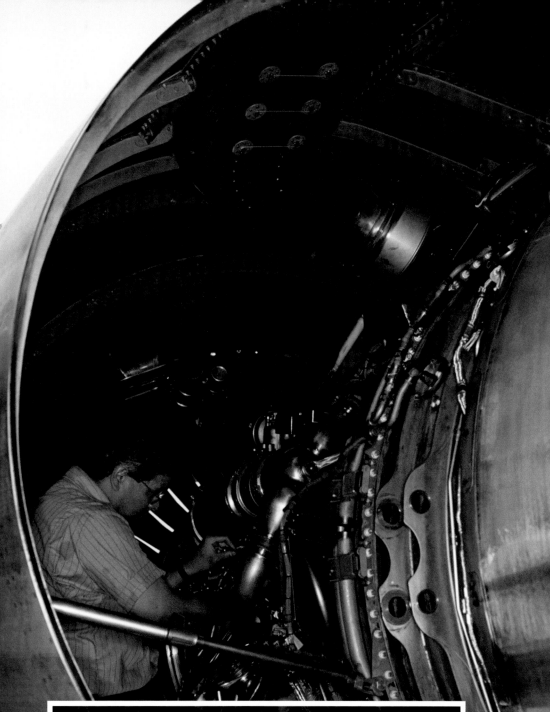

Airplane mechanics ensure that a plane's operating systems are in working order. They examine aircraft frames and parts for defects under strict deadlines.

maintenance inspector. Aircraft mechanics take courses in aircraft electricity, aviation maintenance, aircraft systems, and airframe and power plant mechanics. Advances in computer technology and composite structural material used in new aircraft have made numerous changes in the field of aircraft mechanics.

To get started as an aviation mechanic, you need to have a high school diploma or GED (General Educational Development). The certification you are studying for will determine whether your course will take thirteen, fifteen, or eighteen months. Tuition for the aviation mechanic programs costs between $20,000 and $30,000. Financial aid and grants may be available to qualified students. According to *Aviation Today*, an online publication, an experienced, licensed A&P aviation mechanic has an average salary of $60,000 per year. It should be noted that this is not the salary for an entry-level position as an AMT. New aircraft mechanics will work a forty-hour work week and make around $18 per hour.

There is a high demand for skilled aircraft mechanics. There are two categories of commercial airline mechanics: line maintenance mechanics and overhaul mechanics. Line mechanics work at the airport and make necessary repairs on aircraft between flights. Overhaul mechanics perform scheduled maintenance on the aircraft and conduct inspections required by the FAA. The overhaul mechanics work at an airline's overhaul base hangers. Airline mechanics check for worn or defective parts and determine whether repair or replacement is needed.

AVIONIC EXPERTS

Since the 1970s, aircraft began to incorporate more sophisticated electronic systems onboard. These systems became known as avionics. Flight-control, communication, collision-avoidance, and navigation systems on an airplane account for approximately 40

AIRFRAME AND POWER PLANT (A&P)

There are two major parts of an aircraft: the airframe and the power plant. The airframe includes the fuselage (body of the plane), wings, tail assembly, landing gear, propeller assembly, and fuel and oil tanks. The power plant is the engine radial (internal combustion), turbojet, or turboprop. In order to qualify for an FAA certification in airframe and power plant maintenance, you must have previous work experience as an aircraft mechanic. Many mechanics get this experience through military training. Otherwise, a minimum of eighteen working months for an airframe certificate is required and at least thirty months working on engines is necessary for a power plant certification.

percent of the cost of a new airplane or helicopter. For military aircraft, avionics can account for as much as 80 percent of the budget for equipment. Avionic technicians work on aircraft navigation, weather radar systems, autopilot functions, and communication radios. Therefore, there is a growing need for people who know how these electronic systems work and how to fix them when they are not working properly.

AVIATION SAFETY INSPECTOR

The FAA is responsible for setting rules and regulations to create a safe aviation system. However, enforcement of these regulations is the job of aviation safety inspectors. According to the Department of Transportation Web site, aviation safety inspectors are in charge of developing, administering, and

Aircraft safety begins with proper construction. Safety inspectors are responsible for ensuring that the electronics, among other things, are in proper working order.

enforcing safety regulations and standards for the production, operation, maintenance, or modification of aircraft used in civil aviation.

The FAA identifies eight different types of aviation safety inspectors that specialize in enforcing the FAA safety regulations and standards. Aviation safety inspectors work in one of these three general areas:

1. Aviation safety inspectors working in operations are responsible for certifying pilots, flight instructors, air traffic controllers, and aviation schools. These inspectors must evaluate the people operating the aircraft.

2. The second group of aviation safety inspectors work on the manufacturing end of aircraft safety. They examine the design and materials used in the manufacturing of aircraft.

3. The third area of aviation safety inspectors relates to the mechanics who provide the maintenance, repair, and operation of aircraft equipment. These aviation safety inspectors check maintenance records and flight logs of aircraft. They also certify aviation repair facilities.

All three types of aviation safety inspectors must have good communication skills. A college degree is required for most positions in this field. Many inspectors also have a commercial pilot certificate and a flight instructor certificate. The FAA can arrange for observation opportunities to learn more about what an aviation safety inspector does.

Most aviation safety inspectors work for the federal government, with the FAA and the NTSB. Experienced pilots, aviation engineers, mechanics, technicians, and former air traffic controllers are hired as aviation safety inspectors. These qualified professionals usually start out earning over $43,000 per year. Salaries are based on government salary "grades," which take into account experience, aviation training received, and certificates held by the individual professional being hired.

FAA aviation safety inspectors are the people who investigate airplane accidents. They travel to an aviation accident site and use their knowledge to determine the cause of the accident and what could have been done to prevent it.

Aviation inspectors conduct forensic analysis of aircraft malfunction to discover safety flaws and prevent future malfunctions.

EXPERIMENTAL AIRCRAFT

Experimental aircraft are aircraft that are not approved for flight by the FAA. Homebuilt aircraft and new aerospace technologies fit in this category of aircraft. The Experimental Aircraft Association (EAA) is an organization with chapters in all fifty states. The EAA sponsors many educational programs. For example, its Young Eagles Program gives interested young people ages eight to seventeen an opportunity to fly in a general aviation airplane. Volunteer pilots take these kids for a short flight after explaining the instrumentation of the plane. Each Young Eagle receives a flight log book after his or her first flight. The EAA operates the AirVenture Museum in Oshkosh, Wisconsin. There are summer programs for future aviators to get hands-on experience.

AVIATION SECURITY

The Transportation Security Administration is a federal agency responsible for securing the nation's transportation system. According to its Web site, the TSA operates in 450 airports around the United States. TSA employees are transportation security officers (TSOs), inspectors, directors, air marshals, and managers. It should be noted that 25 percent of the TSA's workforce are veterans of the U.S. military.

TSOs are security screeners. They are the employees responsible for identifying hazardous materials and dangerous objects in baggage, in cargo, and on traveling passengers. The security screeners use specially designed computers, X-ray machines, and handheld scanners to check bags and passengers. These security workers are also trained to detect suspicious behavior and report it to their superiors for additional security checks. The airport checkpoint, although the most visible, is only one level of airport security.

Federal air marshals are responsible for combating threats, such as hostage situations, aboard aircraft. They regularly prepare for all conceivable scenarios.

The Federal Air Marshal Service is part of the TSA, and the federal air marshals (FAMs) are charged with deterring, detecting, and defeating hostile acts targeting U.S. air carriers, airports, passengers and crews. They work closely with other law enforcement officials in keeping the country's civil aviation system safe and secure. Air marshals blend in with travelers and are proficient in handling firearms, interrogation techniques, and homeland security measures.

The Federal Air Marshal Service has twenty-one field offices around the United States, located near major airports. Some TSA security officers are trained to serve as armed security officers (ASO) on flights to Washington, D.C., because of the special security needs surrounding the nation's capital.

The TSA also trains certain eligible flight crew members to become federal flight deck officers. This program gives pilots, flight engineers, and navigators authority to carry firearms in the cockpit and use them in case of an emergency.

All TSA job applicants must complete a written application and have a complete background check before being hired. In addition, federal air marshals must go through a psychological assessment, medical examination, and physical training assessments prior to employment.

TSA career opportunities are available on its Web site. The pay scale for these positions ranges from $17,083 for entry-level jobs to as high as $155,500 in 2011–2012.

chapter 5

SPACE EXPLORATION AND OTHER CAREERS

A stronautics is the study of systems outside Earth's atmosphere. For those who have dreamed of going to space or developing the next mode of transportation to the moon and beyond, a career as a astronautical engineer may be the right choice. Major universities with schools of engineering have programs in astronautical engineering. GPS technology, which allows us to use our smartphones and vehicle navigation systems to find where we are and where we want to go, is an example of how we rely on broadcasting satellites in everyday life.

THE SPACE RACE

On July 29, 1958, President Dwight D. Eisenhower signed the National Aeronautics and Space Act, which created NASA. In the 1960s, the United States and the Soviet Union were involved in the "space race," a competition between the two superpowers for exploration of space. On July 20, 1969, astronaut Neil Armstrong became the first man to set foot on the moon. The *Apollo 11* mission was a huge success for the United States but the *Apollo* missions were very expensive, since the spacecrafts were used only once. In 1981, the first reusable spacecraft, the space shuttle *Columbia*, blasted into space and landed like an

In 2010, President Barack Obama, along with middle school students, congratulated astronauts for their ongoing work aboard the International Space Station.

airplane. The space shuttle could be controlled manually by the crew or remotely by mission control in Houston, Texas. The space shuttle was used to launch equipment in space (including the Hubble Space Telescope) and docked with the Mir Space Station. In 2000, the first crew of American astronauts and Russian cosmonauts arrived at the International Space Station. The last space shuttle landed in July 2011 at the Kennedy Space Center in Florida, officially ending NASA's space shuttle program after thirty years.

On June 28, 2010, President Barack Obama issued the National Space Policy of the United States. It stated that some of the future goals of NASA would be (1) to continue the operations of the International Space Station, (2) implement new space technology development and test programs, and (3) conduct research and development in support of next-generation launch systems. NASA is now focusing on supporting private

THE SMITHSONIAN NATIONAL AIR AND SPACE MUSEUM

The Smithsonian National Air and Space Museum in Washington, D.C., opened on July 1, 1976, and is one of the world's most visited museums. The Smithsonian National Air and Space Museum is filled with aircraft and spacecraft representing the history of aviation and space exploration. At the museum you can learn about the adventurous aviators and astronauts who were the pioneers of flight. You can even see the *Spirit of St. Louis*, the plane flown by Charles Lindbergh in the first nonstop flight from New York to Paris in 1927. College students can apply for an internship at the Air and Space Museum. This is a unique opportunity to learn about the artifacts and materials housed in the Smithsonian's collections.

companies to develop commercial space vehicles that could transport astronauts to the International Space Station.

The FAA's new Office of Commercial Space Transportation (AST) is seeking aerospace engineers and transportation industry analysts to work on future projects in space flight. New jobs are being created to develop regulations and licensing guidelines for the safe operation of commercial space travel. These positions will involve working with aerospace companies in reusable and expendable launch vehicles.

According to the FAA's Web site for the Office of Commercial Space Transportation, these aerospace engineering positions will have an annual salary between $44,827 and $125,943. Note that these jobs require postsecondary degrees in engineering or other technical fields.

There are also opportunities with the AST for candidates who have skills relating to the environmental impact of commercial space transportations vehicles. As these vehicles are being designed and tested, the Environmental Protection Agency will need to be kept informed of how these vehicles impact our environment. Jobs will be created as the need to manage a space transportation system grows in the future.

If you are interested in international affairs and regulatory matters, you may be qualified for a position with the AST International Affairs Program. The goal of this program is to foster a common understanding of and approach to developing internationally consistent operational safety principles and procedures for commercial launch and re-entry operations.

You may choose to work for one of the aerospace companies that are working on designing and testing reusable and expendable launch vehicles. This is the technology of future space travel. NASA and AST are working closely with aerospace companies to advance the U.S. commercial space transportation industry.

The 2011 FAA report "U.S. Commercial Space Transportation Developments and Concepts: Vehicles, Technologies and Spaceports" states that the commercial space transportation industry supports over a million jobs and has a $208 billion impact on the U.S. economy. Therefore, just because the government-sponsored space missions are over does not mean there are no longer jobs in the aerospace industry.

AVIATION FINANCE

The decision whether to purchase or lease aircraft and equipment is a challenging one for airlines. Airlines are in constant need of expensive equipment and new aircraft to keep their fleet updated and safe. Therefore, there is an area of banking

Elon Musk, founder and CEO of SpaceX, a pioneer in the private-sector space exploration industry, discusses the need to create reusable rockets in order to make commercial space travel affordable.

that relates just to aircraft financing. These complex deals involve aircraft manufacturers, airlines, and financial institutions. According to *Airfinance Journal*, a typical aircraft costs $55 million (although very few airlines actually pay this amount). Since airlines don't have that kind of money available when they need to purchase a new plane, they get financing from bank loans or operating leases. If you would like to work in this field, you need to go to college for a business degree to learn about how these financial deals work.

AVIATION MANAGEMENT

Airports are sometimes referred to as beehives. This is because there is so much going on that you see as well as behind the scenes. There are colleges and universities that have majors in aviation management where you learn management principles that keep airports running safely and smoothly. This major includes courses in aviation law, aviation finance, air transportation (understanding the industry), and general business courses such as economics and statistics. Many schools that have programs in aviation management are close to a major airport, and students have the opportunity to do internships with airlines. There is even an international aviation fraternity you can join, Alpha Eta Rho.

Aviation managers are tasked with keeping the flow of commercial aircraft running efficiently and safely at the world's busiest airports.

FOLLOWING THE RIGHT PATH

To decide whether aviation is right for you, first try flying model airplanes or helicopters. The Academy of Model Aeronautics (AMA) is an organization that promotes and teaches about the hobby of model aviation. Flight training

WHO BENEFITS WHEN AIRLINES MERGE?

Over the last several years, some major airlines have merged and become one larger airline. Typically, the merger results in the layoff of employees and a combined reservation system. However, there are numerous businesses that actually profit from airline mergers.

In addition to lawyers, accountants, and computer technicians who make the deal happen, companies that paint planes and put the new logos on seatbacks and airplane terminal signs have to hire employees to handle the extra work.

It costs around $50,000 to paint a small commuter jet plane. According to an article by Hugo Martin for MCT News Service, most commercial aircraft need to be repainted every five years. It takes approximately eleven days to paint a large jet, and the cost to paint a jet of that size is between $100,000 and $200,000.

One of the leading airplane painting companies had to double its workforce and run its operations seven days a week and twenty-four hours a day to handle the merger of United and Continental airlines. The old paint had to be removed, and the planes had to be sanded and prepared for the new paint. It takes about 180 gallons (303 liters) of paint to cover a typical wide-body plane.

programs and instructors are listed on the AMA Web site. It also runs a two-week summer camp for kids who want to learn how to build and fly model aircraft.

How about space camp? Kennedy Space Center in Florida runs summer camp programs for children eight to fourteen years old. Kids work in teams and get to experience the thrill of the space shuttle mission simulators. In addition, the U.S.

Space and Rocket Center in Huntsville, Alabama, has programs for kids starting at seven years old, and there are also adult and family programs. The goal of this camp is to get children interested in aerospace careers and to motivate them to take more science, math, and technology courses.

Another way to explore is to visit one of the many aviation museums around the country. The largest is the Smithsonian National Air and Space Museum in Washington, D.C. The museum has twenty-three galleries exhibiting aircraft, spacecraft, rockets, missiles, and other aviation-related artifacts. There are even online exhibits you can explore to learn about the history of flight and advances in aviation.

The Junior Engineering Technology Society (JETS) offers students opportunities to participate in academic competitions relating to the field of engineering. JETS runs annual activities and has scholarships available to students pursuing a career in engineering.

Students for the Exploration and Development of Space (SEDS) is a nonprofit student group educating future space explorers. It holds high-powered rocketry competitions and publish an informative newsletter.

Finally, if you are sixteen years old, you are eligible to take flying lessons to become a private pilot. A private pilot must first learn to fly a single-engine piston aircraft. Many flight schools around the country have summer flight programs to get you started on earning your wings. You will learn the basics of flight and aerodynamics.

The invention of the airplane and the evolution of modern aviation are monumental human achievements. Air travel has changed the way our world does business and the way we connect with family and different cultures. A career in aviation connects you to the technological and practical advances that will occur in the near future in aircraft, airports, and air safety. Technology will continue to revolutionize air transportation,

Space camp programs allow young people to try their hand at what it's like to be an astronaut. The experience is designed to inspire them to pursue their interests in science, technology, engineering, and math, which are all valuable for careers in aviation.

and there will continue to be a need for talented people to learn the skills to fill the jobs created in the field of aviation.

Certain careers in aviation require specific technical skills or educational degrees. Almost all jobs in aviation in the United States require the candidate to be at least eighteen years old and a U.S. citizen. No matter which area of aviation you choose to pursue, you will be expected to have technical ability, integrity, responsibility, purpose, and a desire to contribute to the strengthening of the profession. As repeatedly emphasized throughout this book, safety is the number one priority for everyone in the aviation industry.

Whether you are looking to travel the world or help others visit sights around the globe, there is a job in aviation, aeronautics, or aerospace for you. You may choose to work directly with the customer or work behind the scenes. Right now, the U.S. air transportation system is experiencing a transformation with innovative new technologies being implemented in aircraft, communications, airport safety and security, and air traffic control. You can be a part of the revolution.

glossary

aerodynamics The study of the properties of moving air around a solid body.

aeronautics The design and operation of any aircraft within Earth's atmosphere.

airframe The body of an aircraft distinct from its engine.

altitude The vertical height above the earth.

astronautics The theory and practice of navigation beyond Earth's atmosphere.

atmosphere The layers of air surrounding Earth.

avionics Electronic systems used on aircraft.

cockpit The enclosed space in the forward part of an airplane fuselage containing the flying controls, instrumentation, and seating for the pilot, copilot, and other flight crew.

DOT The Department of Transportation, a federal agency.

engineer A person who designs, builds, or maintains engines or machines.

FAA The Federal Aviation Administration, a federal agency under the Department of Transportation (DOT).

floatboat A seaplane that takes off and lands on floats in the water.

fuselage The body of an airplane.

International Space Station (ISS) Launched in 1998, the ISS is a man-made, habitable satellite in low-earth orbit designed as a research laboratory where astronauts can conduct a variety of scientific experiments.

National Aeronautics and Space Administration (NASA) The official space agency of the United States, whose mission is to further space exploration and knowledge of the cosmos.

National Transportation Safety Board (NTSB) The independent organization of the United States government tasked with the investigation of transportation accidents.

power plant All the equipment that constitutes a power source.

propulsion A system in an aircraft engine that causes a forward thrust to drive it through the air.

radar A system of using radio waves to navigate or locate objects in the air.

satellite A free-flying object that orbits Earth or another celestial body.

seaplane An aircraft that can take off and land on water.

TSA The Transportation Security Administration.

U.S. Customs and Border Protection (CBP) The Department of Homeland Security agency tasked with securing the nation's borders and monitoring all that enters the country.

Academy of Model Aeronautics (AMA)
5161 E. Memorial Drive
Muncie, IN 47302
(800) 435-9262
Web site: http://www.modelaircraft.org
This model aviation association has over 150,000 members.

Airline Dispatcher Federation (ADF)
2020 Pennsylvania Ave NW, #821
Washington, DC 20006
(800) 676-2685
Web site: http://www.dispatcher.org
This national organization represents the professional interests
    of licensed aircraft dispatch professionals.

Airlines for America (A4A)
1301 Pennsylvania Avenue NW, Suite 1100
Washington, DC 20004
(202) 626-4000
Web site: http://www.airlines.org
This is the trade organization of the principal U.S. airlines.

Airport Consultants Council (ACC)
908 King Street, Suite 100
Alexandria, VA 22314
(703) 683-5900
Web site: http://www.acconline.org

This international trade association represents companies that
provide services to airports and the aviation industry.

Alpha Eta Rho
4579 Laclede Avenue, Suite 1929
St. Louis, MO 63108
(877) 410-1929
Web site: http://www.alphetahro.org
This international aviation fraternity promotes collegiate
aviation leaders.

American Association of Airport Executives (AAAE)
601 Madison Street, Suite 400
Alexandria, VA 22314
(703) 824-0500
Web site: http://www.aaae.org
The AAAE sponsors university campus student chapters that
offer airport management or related aviation degrees.

College Park Aviation Museum
1985 Cpl. Frank Scott Drive
College Park, MD 20740-3836
(877) 444-6777
Web site: http://www.recreation.gov
The College Park Aviation Museum is the world's oldest
continuously operating airport.

Frontiers of Flight Museum
6911 Lemmon Avenue
Dallas, TX 75209
(214) 350-3600

Web site: http://www.flightmuseum.com
The Frontiers of Flight Museum serves to both preserve the
history of aviation while training emerging pilots.

International Air Transport Association
800 Place Victoria
P.O. Box 113
Montreal, QC H4Z 1M1
Canada
(514) 874-0202
Web site: http://www.iata.org
This global trade organization promotes the aviation industry.
It provides internships to college and graduate students.

NASA Glenn Research Center
21000 Brookpark Road
Cleveland, OH 44135
(216) 433-4000
Web site: http://www.grc.nasa.gov
The Glenn Research Center is a division of NASA whose goal
is to advance aeronautics through the exploration of the
solar system and beyond.

Naval Aviation Museum Foundation
1750 Radford Boulevard, Suite B, NAS
Pensacola, FL 32508
Web site: http://www.navalaviationmuseum.org
(850) 452-3604
The National Naval Aviation Museum is the world's largest
Naval Aviation.

Space Exploration Technologies
1 Rocket Road
Hawthorne, CA 90250

(310) 363-6000
Web site: http://www.spacex.com
Founded by Elon Musk, Space Exploration Technologies, also
known as SpaceX, is a private space exploration company.
In May 2012, its Dragon spacecraft made history as the
first commercial spacecraft to visit the International Space
Station.

Teterboro School of Aeronautics
80 Moonachie Avenue
Teterboro, NJ 07608
(201) 288-6300
Web site: http://www.teterboroschool.com
The Teterboro School of Aeronautics has been training pilots
in the New York metropolitan area since 1947.

WEB SITES

Due to the changing nature of Internet links, Rosen Publishing
has developed an online list of Web sites related to the subject
of this book. This site is updated regularly. Please use this link
to access the list:

http://www.rosenlinks.com/ECAR/Avia

for further reading

Bara, Mike. *Dark Mission: The Secret History of NASA*. Port Townsend, WA: Feral House, 2009.

Clegg, Brian. *Inflight Science: A Guide to the World from Your Airplane Window*. London, England: Icon, 2011.

Crane, Dale. *Dictionary of Aeronautics Terms*. Newcastle, WA: Aviation Supplies & Academics, 2006.

Duggins, Pat. *Final Countdown: NASA and the End of the Space Shuttle Program*. Gainesville, FL: University Press of Florida, 2009.

FAR/AIM 2012: Federal Aviation Regulations, Aeronautical Information Manual: Rules and Procedures for General Aviation, Sport Pilots, and Instructors. Newcastle, WA: Aviation Supplies & Academics, 2011.

Federal Aviation Administration. *Pilot's Handbook of Aeronautical Knowledge*. Newcastle, WA: Aviation Supplies & Academics, 2008.

Gardner, Bob. *The Complete Private Pilot*. Newcastle, WA: Aviation Supplies & Academics, 2011.

Hunecke, Klaus. *Jet Engines: Fundamentals of Theory, Design and Operation*. Wiltshire, England: Crowood, 2010.

Kershner, William K. *Student Pilot's Flight Manual: From First Flight to Private Certificate*. Newcastle, WA: Aviation Supplies & Academics, 2010.

Kroes, Michael, et. al. *Aircraft Maintenance and Repair with Study Guide*. New York, NY: McGraw-Hill, 2007.

Laurie, Bobby. *Planely Speaking: Inflight Insight from Thirty Thousand Feet*. Los Angeles, CA: More News Later, LLC, 2011.

Lord, Dick. *From Tailhooker to Mudmover: An Aviation Career in the Royal Air Naval Fleet Air Arm, United States Navy, and South African Air Force.* Johannesburg, South Africa: 30 Degrees South Publishers, 2010.

McCartin, Joseph A. *Collision Course: Ronald Reagan, the Air Traffic Controllers, and the Strike That Changed America.* New York, NY: Oxford University Press, 2011.

Neufeld, Michael J., and Alex M. Spencer. *Smithsonian National Air and Space Museum: An Autobiography.* Washington, D.C.: National Geographic Society, 2010.

Nolan, Michael S. *Fundamentals of Air Traffic Control.* Clifton Park, NY: Delmar, Cengage Learning, 2010.

Rodrigues, Clarence. *Commercial Aviation Safety.* New York, NY: McGraw-Hill, 2011.

Speciale, Raymond. *Fundamentals of Aviation Law.* New York, NY: McGraw-Hill, 2010.

Van Der Linden, Robert F. *The Nation's Hangar: Aircraft Treasures of the Smithsonian from the National Air and Space Museum's Steven F. Udvar-Hazy Center.* Washington, D.C.: Smithsonian, 2011.

bibliography

Air Traffic Control Association. "2012 Navy and Marine Corps ATC Symposium." Retrieved May 30, 2012 (http://www.atca.org).

American Institute of Aeronautics and Astronautics. Retrieved May 30, 2012 (http://www.aiaa.org).

AMT Society. Retrieved May 30, 2012. (http://www.amtsociety.org).

Avjobs.com. Retrieved May 30, 2012 (http://www.avjobs.com).

AvKids.com. Retrieved May 30, 2012 (http://www.avkids.com).

Crouch, Tom D. *Wings: A History of Aviation from Kites to the Space Age.* New York, NY: W. W. Norton & Co., 2003.

Ferguson. *Careers in Focus: Aviation.* New York, NY: Facts On File, 2005.

Gordon, Alastair. *Naked Airport.* New York, NY: Metropolitan Books, 2004.

National Collegiate Inventors and Innovators Alliance (NCIIA). Retrieved May 30, 2012 (http://www.nciia.org).

Rinard, Judith E. *The Smithsonian National Air and Space Museum: Book of Flight.* New York, NY: Firefly Books, 2001.

Smithsonian National Air and Space Museum. Retrieved May 30, 2012. (http://www.airandspace.si.edu).

Space Camp. Retrieved May 30, 2012. (http://www.spacecamp.com).

Szurvoy, Geza. *The American Airport.* St. Paul, MN: MBI Publishing, 2003.

index

A

A&P licensing exams, 44
Academy of Model Aeronautics, 63–64
aerodynamicists, 36, 38
aerospace engineers, 6, 8, 36–43
Aircraft Rescue and Firefighting
(ARFF) Training Academy, 30
Airfinance Journal, 61
airframe and power plant (A&P),
44, 47
Airline Dispatchers Federation, 43
airline mergers, 64
air marshals, 52, 54
air traffic controllers, 5, 8–9, 23–27,
49, 50
Air Traffic Control System
Command Center, 24
AirVenture Museum, 52
Alpha Eta Rho, 62
American Airport, The, 21
American Institute of Aeronautics
and Astronautics (AIAA), 40
Apollo 11, 55
Armstrong, Neil, 55
ATC computer specialists, 30
AT-CTI programs, 23
attendants, flight, 7, 18–20
aviation careers
aerospace, 6, 8, 36–43, 55–59, 65
airport, 5, 21–35
finance, 59–61

jobs in the air, 5, 8–20
maintenance, 5, 6, 27, 44–52
management, 5, 61–62
overview, 4–7, 63–67
security, 5, 25, 34–35, 52–54
Aviation High School, 39–40
aviation maintenance technicians,
44, 46
Aviation Today, 46
avionic experts, 46–47

B

background checks, 20, 54
baggage/cargo handlers, 27, 28–29
Bureau of Labor Statistics, 19

C

cabin service workers, 28
Civil Aviation Act of 1938, 22
Civil Aviation Authority (CAA), 22
civil service exams, 23
Code of Federal Regulations, 9
Columbia, 55
concessions workers, 31
copilots, 5, 17
customs officials, 34–35

D

Denver International Airport, 30, 31
dispatchers, 42–43
Douglas DC-3, 21

ABOUT THE AUTHOR

Suzanne Weinick graduated from the University at Albany, State University of New York with a B.A. in political science. She went on to Hofstra University School of Law and practiced corporate law full-time until she became a mom. She now practices law part-time and enjoys writing books for tweens and teens. Her husband, Jeff, has built and flown model airplanes and would love to get his private pilot's license. She has an eighteen-year-old daughter and sixteen-year-old son who enjoying traveling with her.

PHOTO CREDITS

Cover (pilot) Peter Dazeley/Riser/Getty Images; cover (background), p. 1 Digital Vision/Thinkstock; pp. 4–5, 60–61 Bloomberg/Getty Images; pp. 10–11 Digital Vision/Photodisc/Thinkstock; pp. 12–13 Alberto Incrocci/The Image Bank/Getty Images; pp. 16–17 Bruce Dale/National Geographic Image Collection/Getty Images; pp. 18–19 Westend61/Getty Images; pp. 22–23 Monty Rakusen/Cultura/Getty Images; pp. 26–27 ChinaFotoPress/Getty Images; pp. 28–29 Lester Lefkowitz/Stone/Getty Images; pp. 32–33 Digital Vision/Thinkstock; pp. 34, 52–53 © AP Images; p. 37 Gilles Rolle/REA/Redux; pp. 40–41 © Jack Kurtz/Zuma Press; p. 45 Kim Steele/Photodisc/Thinkstock; pp. 48–49 Patrick Landmann/Photo Researchers, Inc.; pp. 50–51 © St. Petersburg Times/Zuma Press; pp. 56–57 Getty Images; pp. 62–63 © imagebroker.net/SuperStock; p. 66 © Michael J. Doolittle/The Image Works; back cover © istockphoto.com/blackred.

Designer: Matt Cauli; Editor: Nicholas Croce;
Photo Researcher: Marty Levick